On the Eucharist

ON THE EUCHARIST

POPE JOHN PAUL II

Our Sunday Visitor
Huntington, Indiana

Published by Our Sunday Visitor

28 27 26 25 24 23   1 2 3 4 5 6 7 8 9

Our Sunday Visitor Publishing Division, Our Sunday Visitor, Inc., 200 Noll Plaza, Huntington, IN 46750; 1-800-348-2440; www.osv.com

ISBN: 978-1-63966-135-0 (Inventory No. T2852)
eISBN: 978-1-63966-136-7
LCCN: 2023938974

Cover design: Tyler Ottinger
Cover art: AdobeStock
Interior design: Amanda Falk

PRINTED IN THE UNITED STATES OF AMERICA

TABLE OF CONTENTS

INTRODUCTION

1. The Church draws her life from the Eucharist. This truth does not simply express a daily experience of faith but recapitulates *the heart of the mystery of the Church.* In a variety of ways, she joyfully experiences the constant fulfilment of the promise: "Lo, I am with you always, to the close of the age" (Mt 28:20), but in the holy Eucharist, through the changing of bread and wine into the Body and Blood of the Lord, she rejoices in this presence with unique intensity. Ever since Pentecost, when the Church, the People of the New Covenant, began her pilgrim journey toward her heavenly homeland, the Divine Sacrament has continued to mark the passing of her days, filling them with confident hope.

The Second Vatican Council rightly proclaimed that the Eucharistic sacrifice is "the source and summit of the Christian life."[1] "For the most holy Eucharist contains the Church's entire spiritual wealth: Christ himself, our passover and living bread. Through his own flesh, now made living and life-giving by the Holy Spirit, he offers life to men."[2] Consequently the gaze of the Church is constantly turned to her Lord, present in the Sacrament of the Altar, in which she discovers the full manifestation of his boundless love.

2. During the Great Jubilee of the Year 2000 I had an opportunity to celebrate the Eucharist in the Cenacle of Jerusalem where, according to tradition, it was first celebrated by Jesus himself. *The Upper Room was where*

7

this most holy Sacrament was instituted. It is there that Christ took bread, broke it, and gave it to his disciples, saying, "Take this, all of you, and eat it: this is my body which will be given up for you" (cf. Mt 26:26; Lk 22:19; 1 Cor 11:24). Then he took the cup of wine and said to them: "Take this, all of you and drink from it: this is the cup of my blood, the blood of the new and everlasting covenant. It will be shed for you and for all, so that sins may be forgiven" (cf. Mk 14:24; Lk 22:20; 1 Cor 11:25). I am grateful to the Lord Jesus for allowing me to repeat in that same place, in obedience to his command, "Do this in memory of me" (Lk 22:19), the words which he spoke two thousand years ago.

Did the apostles who took part in the Last Supper understand the meaning of the words spoken by Christ? Perhaps not. Those words would only be fully clear at the end of the *Triduum sacrum*, the time from Thursday evening to Sunday morning. Those days embrace the *mysterium paschale*; they also embrace the *mysterium eucharisticum.*

3. The Church was born of the paschal mystery. For this very reason the Eucharist, which is in an outstanding way the sacrament of the paschal mystery, *stands at the center of the Church's life.* This is already clear from the earliest images of the Church found in the Acts of the Apostles: "They devoted themselves to the apostles' teaching and fellowship, to the breaking of bread and the prayers" (2:42). The "breaking of the bread" refers to the Eucharist. Two thousand years later, we continue to relive that primordial image of the Church. At every

celebration of the Eucharist, we are spiritually brought back to the paschal Triduum: to the events of the evening of Holy Thursday, to the Last Supper, and to what followed it. The institution of the Eucharist sacramentally anticipated the events which were about to take place, beginning with the agony in Gethsemane. Once again we see Jesus as he leaves the Upper Room, descends with his disciples to the Kidron valley and goes to the Garden of Olives. Even today that garden shelters some very ancient olive trees. Perhaps they witnessed what happened beneath their shade that evening, when Christ in prayer was filled with anguish "and his sweat became like drops of blood falling down upon the ground" (cf. Lk 22:44). The blood which shortly before he had given to the Church as the drink of salvation in the Sacrament of the Eucharist, *began to be shed*; its outpouring would then be completed on Golgotha to become the means of our redemption: "Christ ... as high priest of the good things to come ... entered once for all into the Holy Place, taking not the blood of goats and calves but his own blood, thus securing an eternal redemption" (Heb 9:11–12).

4. *The hour of our redemption.* Although deeply troubled, Jesus does not flee before his "hour." "And what shall I say? 'Father, save me from this hour?' No, for this purpose I have come to this hour" (Jn 12:27). He wanted his disciples to keep him company, yet he had to experience loneliness and abandonment: "So, could you not watch with me one hour? Watch and pray that you may not enter into temptation" (Mt 26:40–41). Only John would remain at the foot of the cross, at the side of Mary

and the faithful women. The agony in Gethsemane was the introduction to the agony of the cross on Good Friday. *The holy hour,* the hour of the redemption of the world. Whenever the Eucharist is celebrated at the tomb of Jesus in Jerusalem, there is an almost tangible return to his "hour," the hour of his cross and glorification. Every priest who celebrates holy Mass, together with the Christian community which takes part in it, is led back in spirit to that place and that hour.

"He was crucified, he suffered death and was buried; he descended to the dead; on the third day he rose again." The words of the profession of faith are echoed by the words of contemplation and proclamation: *"This is the wood of the cross, on which hung the Savior of the world. Come, let us worship."* This is the invitation which the Church extends to all in the afternoon hours of Good Friday. She then takes up her song during the Easter season in order to proclaim, *"The Lord is risen from the tomb; for our sake he hung on the cross. Alleluia."*

5. *"Mysterium fidei!* — The Mystery of Faith!" When the priest recites or chants these words, all present acclaim, "We announce your death, O Lord, and we proclaim your resurrection, until you come in glory."

In these or similar words the Church, while pointing to Christ in the mystery of his passion, *also reveals her own mystery: Ecclesia de Eucharistia.* By the gift of the Holy Spirit at Pentecost the Church was born and set out upon the pathways of the world, yet a decisive moment in her taking shape was certainly the institution of the Eucharist in the Upper Room. Her foundation and wellspring is the whole *Triduum paschale*, but this is as it were gathered up, foreshadowed and "concentrated" forever in the gift of the Eucharist. In this gift Jesus Christ entrusted to his Church the perennial making present of the Paschal Mystery. With it he brought about a mysterious "oneness in time" between that *Triduum* and the passage of the centuries.

The thought of this leads us to profound amazement and gratitude. In the paschal event and the Eucharist which makes it present throughout the centuries, there is a truly enormous "capacity" which embraces all of history as the recipient of the grace of the redemption. This amazement should always fill the Church assembled for the celebration of the Eucharist. But in a special way it should fill the minister of the Eucharist. For it is he who, by the authority given him in the sacrament of priestly ordination, effects the consecration. It is he who says with the power coming to him from Christ in the Upper Room: "This is my body which will be given up for you. This is the cup of my blood, poured out for you." The priest says these words, or rather *he puts his voice at the disposal of the One who spoke these words in the Upper Room* and who desires that they should be repeated in every generation by all those who in the Church ministerially share in his priesthood.

6. I would like to rekindle this Eucharistic "amazement" by the present encyclical letter, in continuity with the Jubilee heritage which I have left to the Church in the apostolic letter *Novo Millennio Ineunte* and its Marian

crowning, *Rosarium Virginis Mariae*. To contemplate the face of Christ, and to contemplate it with Mary, is the "program" which I have set before the Church at the dawn of the third millennium, summoning her to put out into the deep on the sea of history with the enthusiasm of the New Evangelization. To contemplate Christ involves being able to recognize him wherever he manifests himself, in his many forms of presence, but above all in the living sacrament of his Body and his Blood. *The Church draws her life from Christ in the Eucharist*; by him she is fed and by him she is enlightened. The Eucharist is both a mystery of faith and a "mystery of light."[3] Whenever the Church celebrates the Eucharist, the faithful can in some way relive the experience of the two disciples on the road to Emmaus: "their eyes were opened and they recognized him" (Lk 24:31).

7. From the time I began my ministry as the successor of Peter, I have always marked Holy Thursday, the day of the Eucharist and of the priesthood, by sending a letter to all the priests of the world. This year, the twenty-fifth of my pontificate, I wish to involve the whole Church more fully in this Eucharistic reflection, also as a way of thanking the Lord for the gift of the Eucharist and the priesthood: "Gift and Mystery."[4] By proclaiming the Year of the Rosary, I wish to put this, my twenty-fifth anniversary, *under the aegis of the contemplation of Christ at the school of Mary.* Consequently, I cannot let this Holy Thursday 2003 pass without halting before the "Eucharistic face" of Christ and pointing out with new force to the Church the centrality of the Eucharist.

From it the Church draws her life. From this "living bread" she draws her nourishment. How could I not feel the need to urge everyone to experience it ever anew?

8. When I think of the Eucharist, and look at my life as a priest, as a bishop and as the successor of Peter, I naturally recall the many times and places in which I was able to celebrate it. I remember the parish church of Niegowić, where I had my first pastoral assignment, the collegiate church of Saint Florian in Kraków, Wawel Cathedral, Saint Peter's Basilica, and so many basilicas and churches in Rome and throughout the world. I have been able to celebrate holy Mass in chapels built along mountain paths, on lakeshores and seacoasts; I have celebrated it on altars built in stadiums and in city squares. This varied scenario of celebrations of the Eucharist has given me a powerful experience of its universal and, so to speak, cosmic character. Yes, cosmic! Because even when it is celebrated on the humble altar of a country church, the Eucharist is always in some way celebrated *on the altar of the world*. It unites heaven and earth. It embraces and permeates all creation. The Son of God became man in order to restore all creation, in one supreme act of praise, to the One who made it from nothing. He, the Eternal High Priest who by the blood of his cross entered the eternal sanctuary, thus gives back to the Creator and Father all creation redeemed. He does so through the priestly ministry of the Church, to the glory of the Most Holy Trinity. Truly this is the *mysterium fidei* which is accomplished in the Eucharist: the world which came forth from the hands of God the Creator now returns to him redeemed by Christ.

9. The Eucharist, as Christ's saving presence in the community of the faithful and its spiritual food, is the most precious possession which the Church can have in her journey through history. This explains the *lively concern* which she has always shown for the Eucharistic mystery, a concern which finds authoritative expression in the work of the councils and the popes. How can we not admire the doctrinal expositions of the decrees on the Most Holy Eucharist and on the Holy Sacrifice of the Mass promulgated by the Council of Trent? For centuries those decrees guided theology and catechesis, and they are still a dogmatic reference point for the continual renewal and growth of God's people in faith and in love for the Eucharist. In times closer to our own, three encyclical letters should be mentioned: *Mirae Caritatis* of Leo XIII (May 28, 1902),[5] *Mediator Dei* of Pius XII (November 20, 1947),[6] and *Mysterium Fidei* of Paul VI (September 3, 1965).[7]

The Second Vatican Council, while not issuing a specific document on the Eucharistic mystery, considered its various aspects throughout its documents, especially the Dogmatic Constitution on the Church, *Lumen Gentium*, and the Constitution on the Sacred Liturgy, *Sacrosanctum Concilium*.

I myself, in the first years of my apostolic ministry in the Chair of Peter, wrote the apostolic letter *Dominicae Cenae* (February 24, 1980),[8] in which I discussed some aspects of the Eucharistic mystery and its importance for the life of those who are its ministers. Today I take up anew the thread of that argument, with even greater emotion and gratitude in my heart, echoing as it were the word of the psalmist: "What shall I render to the LORD / for all his bounty to me? / I will lift up the cup of salvation / and call on the name of the LORD" (Ps 116:12–13).

10. The Magisterium's commitment to proclaiming the Eucharistic mystery has been matched by interior growth within the Christian community. Certainly, *the liturgical reform inaugurated by the council* has greatly contributed to a more conscious, active, and fruitful participation in the Holy Sacrifice of the Altar on the part of the faithful. In many places, *adoration of the Blessed Sacrament* is also an important daily practice and becomes an inexhaustible source of holiness. The devout participation of the faithful in the Eucharistic procession on the Solemnity of the Body and Blood of Christ is a grace from the Lord which yearly brings joy to those who take part in it.

Other positive signs of Eucharistic faith and love might also be mentioned.

Unfortunately, alongside these lights, *there are also shadows*. In some places the practice of Eucharistic adoration has been almost completely abandoned. In various parts of the Church abuses have occurred, leading to confusion with regard to sound faith and Catholic doctrine concerning this wonderful sacrament. At times one encounters an extremely reductive understanding of the Eucharistic mystery. Stripped of its sacrificial meaning, it is celebrated as if it were simply a fraternal banquet. Furthermore, the necessity of the ministerial priesthood, grounded in apostolic succession, is at times obscured and the sacramental nature of the Eucharist is reduced to its mere effectiveness as a form of proclamation. This has led here and there to ecumenical initiatives which, albeit well-intentioned, indulge in Eucharistic practices contrary to the discipline by which the Church expresses her Faith. How can we not express profound grief at all this? The Eucharist is too great a gift to tolerate ambiguity and depreciation.

It is my hope that the present encyclical letter will effectively help to banish the dark clouds of unacceptable doctrine and practice, so that the Eucharist will continue to shine forth in all its radiant mystery.

THE MYSTERY OF FAITH

11. "The Lord Jesus on the night he was betrayed" (1 Cor 11:23) instituted the Eucharistic Sacrifice of his Body and his Blood. The words of the apostle Paul bring us back to the dramatic setting in which the Eucharist was born. The Eucharist is indelibly marked by the event of the Lord's passion and death, of which it is not only a reminder but the sacramental re-presentation. It is the sacrifice of the cross perpetuated down the ages.[9] This truth is well expressed by the words with which the assembly in the Latin rite responds to the priest's proclamation of the "Mystery of Faith": *"We announce your death, O Lord."*

The Church has received the Eucharist from Christ her Lord not as one gift — however precious — among so many others, but as *the gift par excellence*, for it is the gift of himself, of his person in his sacred humanity, as well as the gift of his saving work. Nor does it remain confined to the past, since "all that Christ is — all that he did and suffered for all men — participates in the divine eternity, and so transcends all times."[10]

When the Church celebrates the Eucharist, the memorial of her Lord's death and resurrection, this central event of salvation becomes really present and "the work of our redemption is carried out."[11] This sacrifice is so decisive for the salvation of the human race that Jesus

Christ offered it and returned to the Father only *after he had left us a means of sharing in it* as if we had been present there. Each member of the faithful can thus take part in it and inexhaustibly gain its fruits. This is the faith from which generations of Christians down the ages have lived. The Church's Magisterium has constantly reaffirmed this faith with joyful gratitude for its inestimable gift.[12] I wish once more to recall this truth and to join you, my dear brothers and sisters, in adoration before this mystery: a great mystery, a mystery of mercy. What more could Jesus have done for us? Truly, in the Eucharist, he shows us a love which goes "to the end" (cf. Jn 13:1), a love which knows no measure.

12. This aspect of the universal charity of the Eucharistic Sacrifice is based on the words of the Savior himself. In instituting it, he did not merely say: "This is my body," "this is my blood," but went on to add: "which is given for you," "which is poured out for you" (Lk 22:19–20). Jesus did not simply state that what he was giving them to eat and drink was his Body and his Blood; he also expressed *its sacrificial meaning* and made sacramentally present his sacrifice which would soon be offered on the cross for the salvation of all. "The Mass is at the same time, and inseparably, the sacrificial memorial in which the sacrifice of the Cross is perpetuated and the sacred banquet of communion with the Lord's body and blood."[13]

The Church constantly draws her life from the redeeming sacrifice; she approaches it not only through faith-filled remembrance, but also through a real contact, since *this sacrifice is made present ever anew*, sacramentally perpetuated, in every community which offers it at the hands of the consecrated minister. The Eucharist thus applies to men and women today the reconciliation won once for all by Christ for mankind in every age. "The sacrifice of Christ and the sacrifice of the Eucharist are *one single sacrifice*."[14] St. John Chrysostom put it well: "We always offer the same Lamb, not one today and another tomorrow, but always the same one. For this reason the sacrifice is always only one. ... Even now we offer that victim who was once offered and who will never be consumed."[15]

The Mass makes present the sacrifice of the cross; it does not add to that sacrifice, nor does it multiply it.[16] What is repeated is its *memorial* celebration, its "commemorative representation" (*memorialis demonstratio*),[17] which makes Christ's one, definitive redemptive sacrifice always present in time. The sacrificial nature of the Eucharistic mystery cannot therefore be understood as something separate, independent of the cross or only indirectly referring to the sacrifice of Calvary.

13. By virtue of its close relationship to the sacrifice of Golgotha, the Eucharist is *a sacrifice in the strict sense*, and not only in a general way, as if it were simply a matter of Christ's offering himself to the faithful as their spiritual food. The gift of his love and obedience to the point of giving his life (cf. *Jn* 10:17–18) is in the first place a gift to his Father. Certainly it is a gift given for our sake, and indeed that of all humanity (cf. Mt 26:28; Mk 14:24; Lk 22:20; Jn 10:15), yet it is *first and foremost a gift to the*

Father: "a sacrifice that the Father accepted, giving, in return for this total self-giving by his Son, who 'became obedient unto death' (Phil 2:8), his own paternal gift, that is to say the grant of new immortal life in the resurrection."[18]

In giving his sacrifice to the Church, Christ has also made his own the spiritual sacrifice of the Church, which is called to offer herself in union with the sacrifice of Christ. This is the teaching of the Second Vatican Council concerning all the faithful: "Taking part in the Eucharistic Sacrifice, which is the source and summit of the whole Christian life, they offer the divine victim to God, and offer themselves along with it."[19]

14. Christ's passover includes not only his passion and death, but also his resurrection. This is recalled by the assembly's acclamation following the consecration: *"We proclaim your resurrection."* The Eucharistic Sacrifice makes present not only the mystery of the Savior's passion and death, but also the mystery of the Resurrection which crowned his sacrifice. It is as the living and risen One that Christ can become in the Eucharist the "bread of life" (Jn 6:35, 48), the "living bread" (Jn 6:51). Saint Ambrose reminded the newly initiated that the Eucharist applies the event of the Resurrection to their lives: "Today Christ is yours, yet each day he rises again for you."[20] St. Cyril of Alexandria also makes clear that sharing in the sacred mysteries "is a true confession and a remembrance that the Lord died and returned to life for us and on our behalf."[21]

15. The sacramental re-presentation of Christ's sacrifice, crowned by the Resurrection, in the Mass involves a most special presence which — in the words of Paul VI — "is called 'real' not as a way of excluding all other types of presence as if they were 'not real,' but because it is a presence in the fullest sense: a substantial presence whereby Christ, the God-Man, is wholly and entirely present."[22] This sets forth once more the perennially valid teaching of the Council of Trent: "The consecration of the bread and wine effects the change of the whole substance of the bread into the substance of the body of Christ our Lord, and of the whole substance of the wine into the substance of his blood. And the holy Catholic Church has fittingly and properly called this change transubstantiation."[23] Truly the Eucharist is a *mysterium fidei*, a mystery which surpasses our understanding and can only be received in faith, as is often brought out in the catechesis of the Church Fathers regarding this divine sacrament: "Do not see — St. Cyril of Jerusalem exhorts — in the bread and wine merely natural elements, because the Lord has expressly said that they are his body and his blood: faith assures you of this, though your senses suggest otherwise."[24]

Adoro te devote, latens Deitas, we shall continue to sing with the Angelic Doctor (St. Thomas Aquinas). Before this mystery of love, human reason fully experiences its limitations. One understands how, down the centuries, this truth has stimulated theology to strive to understand it ever more deeply.

These are praiseworthy efforts, which are all the more

helpful and insightful to the extent that they are able to join critical thinking to the "living faith" of the Church, as grasped especially by the Magisterium's "sure charism of truth" and the "intimate sense of spiritual realities"[25] which is attained above all by the saints. There remains the boundary indicated by Paul VI: "Every theological explanation which seeks some understanding of this mystery, in order to be in accord with Catholic faith, must firmly maintain that in objective reality, independently of our mind, the bread and wine have ceased to exist after the consecration, so that the adorable body and blood of the Lord Jesus from that moment on are really before us under the sacramental species of bread and wine."[26]

16. The saving efficacy of the sacrifice is fully realized when the Lord's Body and Blood are received in Communion. The Eucharistic Sacrifice is intrinsically directed to the inward union of the faithful with Christ through Communion; we receive the very One who offered himself for us, we receive his Body which he gave up for us on the cross and his Blood which he "poured out for many for the forgiveness of sins" (Mt 26:28). We are reminded of his words: "As the living Father sent me, and I live because of the Father, so he who eats me will live because of me" (Jn 6:57). Jesus himself reassures us that this union, which he compares to that of the life of the Trinity, is truly realized. *The Eucharist is a true banquet*, in which Christ offers himself as our nourishment. When for the first time Jesus spoke of this food, his listeners were astonished and bewildered, which forced the Master to emphasize the objective truth of

his words: "Truly, truly, I say to you, unless you eat the flesh of the Son of Man and drink his blood, you have no life within you" (Jn 6:53). This is no metaphorical food: "My flesh is food indeed, and my blood is drink indeed" (Jn 6:55).

17. Through our communion in his Body and Blood, Christ also grants us his Spirit. Saint Ephrem writes: "He called the bread his living body and he filled it with himself and his Spirit. ... He who eats it with faith, eats Fire and Spirit. ... Take and eat this, all of you, and eat with it the Holy Spirit. For it is truly my body and who-ever eats it will have eternal life."[27] The Church implores this divine Gift, the source of every other gift, in the Eucharistic epiclesis. In the *Divine Liturgy* of St. John Chrysostom, for example, we find the prayer, "We be-seech, implore and beg you: send your Holy Spirit upon us all and upon these gifts ... that those who partake of them may be purified in soul, receive the forgive-ness of their sins, and share in the Holy Spirit."[28] And in the *Roman Missal* the celebrant prays, "Grant that we who are nourished by his body and blood may be filled with his Holy Spirit, and become one body, one spirit in Christ."[29] Thus by the gift of his body and blood Christ increases within us the gift of his Spirit, already poured out in baptism and bestowed as a "seal" in the Sacra-ment of Confirmation.

18. The acclamation of the assembly following the con-secration appropriately ends by expressing the escha-tological thrust which marks the celebration of the Eu-charist (cf. 1 Cor 11:26): *"until you come in glory."* The

Eucharist is a straining toward the goal, a foretaste of the fullness of joy promised by Christ (cf. Jn 15:11); it is in some way the anticipation of heaven, the "pledge of future glory."[30] In the Eucharist, everything speaks of confident waiting "in joyful hope for the coming of our Savior, Jesus Christ."[31] Those who feed on Christ in the Eucharist need not wait until the hereafter to receive eternal life: *they already possess it on earth*, as the first-fruits of a future fullness which will embrace man in his totality. For in the Eucharist we also receive the pledge of our bodily resurrection at the end of the world: "He who eats my flesh and drinks my blood has eternal life, and I will raise him up at the last day" (Jn 6:54). This pledge of the future resurrection comes from the fact that the flesh of the Son of Man, given as food, is his Body in its glorious state after the Resurrection. With the Eucharist we digest, as it were, the "secret" of the Resurrection. For this reason St. Ignatius of Antioch rightly defined the Eucharistic Bread as "a medicine of immortality, an antidote to death."[32]

19. The eschatological tension kindled by the Eucharist *expresses and reinforces our communion with the Church in heaven*. It is not by chance that the Eastern Anaphoras and the Latin Eucharistic prayers honor Mary, the ever-Virgin Mother of Jesus Christ our Lord and God, the angels, the holy apostles, the glorious martyrs, and all the saints. This is an aspect of the Eucharist which merits greater attention: In celebrating the sacrifice of the Lamb, we are united to the heavenly "liturgy" and become part of that great multitude which cries out, "Salvation belongs to our God who sits upon

the throne, and to the Lamb!" (Rv 7:10). The Eucharist is truly a glimpse of heaven appearing on earth. It is a glorious ray of the heavenly Jerusalem which pierces the clouds of our history and lights up our journey.

20. A significant consequence of the eschatological tension inherent in the Eucharist is also the fact that it spurs us on our journey through history and plants a seed of living hope in our daily commitment to the work before us. Certainly, the Christian vision leads to the expectation of "new heavens" and "a new earth" (Rv 21:1), but this increases, rather than lessens, *our sense of responsibility for the world today*.[33] I wish to reaffirm this forcefully at the beginning of the new millennium, so that Christians will feel more obliged than ever not to neglect their duties as citizens in this world. Theirs is the task of contributing with the light of the Gospel to the building of a more human world, a world fully in harmony with God's plan.

Many problems darken the horizon of our time. We need but think of the urgent need to work for peace, to base relationships between peoples on solid premises of justice and solidarity, and to defend human life from conception to its natural end. And what should we say of the thousand inconsistencies of a "globalized" world where the weakest, the most powerless, and the poorest appear to have so little hope! It is in this world that Christian hope must shine forth! For this reason, too, the Lord wished to remain with us in the Eucharist, making his presence in meal and sacrifice the promise of a humanity renewed by his love. Significantly, in their account of the Last Supper, the Synoptic [Gospels] recount the institution of the Eucharist, while the Gospel of John relates, as a way of bringing out its profound meaning, the account of the "washing of the feet," in which Jesus appears as the teacher of communion and of service (cf. Jn 13:1-20). The apostle Paul, for his part, says that it is "unworthy" of a Christian community to partake of the Lord's Supper amid division and indifference toward the poor (cf. 1 Cor 11:17-22, 27-34).[34]

Proclaiming the death of the Lord "until he comes" (1 Cor 11:26) entails that all who take part in the Eucharist be committed to changing their lives and making them in a certain way completely "Eucharistic." It is this fruit of a transfigured existence and a commitment to transforming the world in accordance with the Gospel which splendidly illustrates the eschatological tension inherent in the celebration of the Eucharist and in the Christian life as a whole: "Come, Lord Jesus!" (Rv 22:20).

THE EUCHARIST BUILDS THE CHURCH

21. The Second Vatican Council teaches that the celebration of the Eucharist is at the center of the process of the Church's growth. After stating that "the Church, as the Kingdom of Christ already present in mystery, grows visibly in the world through the power of God,"[35] then, as if in answer to the question, "How does the Church grow?", the council adds, "As often as the sacrifice of the Cross by which 'Christ our pasch is sacrificed' (1 Cor 5:7) is celebrated on the altar, the work of our redemption is carried out. At the same time in the sacrament of the Eucharistic bread, the unity of the faithful, who form one body in Christ (cf. 1 Cor 10:17), is both expressed and brought about."[36]

A causal influence of the Eucharist is present at the Church's very origins. The evangelists specify that it was the Twelve, the apostles, who gathered with Jesus at the Last Supper (cf. Mt 26:20; Mk 14:17; Lk 22:14). This is a detail of notable importance, for the apostles "were both the seeds of the new Israel and the beginning of the sacred hierarchy."[37] By offering them his Body and his Blood as food, Christ mysteriously involved them in the sacrifice which would be completed later on Calvary. By analogy with the Covenant of Mount Sinai, sealed by sacrifice and the sprinkling of blood,[38] the actions and words of Jesus at the Last Supper laid the foundations of the new messianic community, the People of the New Covenant.

The apostles, by accepting in the Upper Room Jesus' invitation: "Take, eat" [and] "Drink of it, all of you" (Mt 26:26–27), entered for the first time into sacramental communion with him. From that time forward, until the end of the age, the Church is built up through sacramental communion with the Son of God who was sacrificed for our sake: "Do this is remembrance of me. ... Do this, as often as you drink it, in remembrance of me" (1 Cor 11:24–25; cf. Lk 22:19).

22. Incorporation into Christ, which is brought about by baptism, is constantly renewed and consolidated by sharing in the Eucharistic Sacrifice, especially by that full sharing which takes place in sacramental communion. We can say not only that *each of us receives Christ*, but also that *Christ receives each of us*. He enters into friendship with us: "You are my friends" (Jn 15:14). Indeed, it is because of him that we have life: "He who eats me will live because of me" (Jn 6:57). Eucharistic communion brings about in a sublime way the mutual "abiding" of Christ and each of his followers: "Abide in me, and I in you" (Jn 15:4).

By its union with Christ, the People of the New Covenant, far from closing in upon itself, becomes a "sacrament" for humanity,[39] a sign and instrument of the salvation achieved by Christ, the light of the world and the salt of the earth (cf. Mt 5:13–16), for the redemption of all.[40] The Church's mission stands in continuity with the mission of Christ: "As the Father has sent me, even so I send you" (Jn 20:21). From the perpetuation of the sacrifice of the cross and her communion with the Body and Blood of Christ in the Eucharist, the Church draws the spiritual power needed to carry out her mission. The Eucharist thus appears as both *the source* and *the summit* of all evangelization, since its goal is the communion of mankind with Christ and in him with the Father and the Holy Spirit.[41]

23. Eucharistic communion also confirms the Church in her unity as the body of Christ. Saint Paul refers to this *unifying power* of participation in the banquet of the Eucharist when he writes to the Corinthians: "The bread which we break, is it not a communion in the body of Christ? Because there is one bread, we who are many are one body, for we all partake of the one bread" (1 Cor 10:16-17). St. John Chrysostom's commentary on these words is profound and perceptive: "For what is the bread? It is the body of Christ. And what do those who receive it become? The Body of Christ — not many bodies but one body. For as bread is completely one, though made up of many grains of wheat, and these, albeit unseen, remain nonetheless present, in such a way that their difference is not apparent since they have been made a perfect whole, so too are we mutually joined to one another and together united with Christ."[42] The argument is compelling: Our union with Christ, which is a gift and grace for each of us, makes it possible for us, in him, to share in the unity of his body which is the Church. The Eucharist reinforces the incorporation into

Christ which took place in baptism through the gift of the Spirit (cf. 1 Cor 12:13, 27).

The joint and inseparable activity of the Son and of the Holy Spirit, which is at the origin of the Church, of her consolidation and her continued life, is at work in the Eucharist. This was clearly evident to the author of the *Liturgy of Saint James*: in the epiclesis of the Anaphora, God the Father is asked to send the Holy Spirit upon the faithful and upon the offerings, so that the Body and Blood of Christ "may be a help to all those who partake of it ... for the sanctification of their souls and bodies."[43] The Church is fortified by the divine Paraclete through the sanctification of the faithful in the Eucharist.

24. The gift of Christ and his Spirit which we receive in Eucharistic communion superabundantly fulfills the yearning for fraternal unity deeply rooted in the human heart; at the same time, it elevates the experience of fraternity already present in our common sharing at the same Eucharistic table to a degree which far surpasses that of the simple human experience of sharing a meal. Through her communion with the Body of Christ the Church comes to be ever more profoundly "in Christ in the nature of a sacrament, that is, a sign and instrument of intimate unity with God and of the unity of the whole human race."[44]

The seeds of disunity, which daily experience shows to be so deeply rooted in humanity as a result of sin, are countered by *the unifying power* of the Body of Christ.

The Eucharist, precisely by building up the Church, creates human community.

25. The *worship of the Eucharist outside of the Mass* is of inestimable value for the life of the Church. This worship is strictly linked to the celebration of the Eucharistic Sacrifice. The presence of Christ under the Sacred Species reserved after Mass — a presence which lasts as long as the species of bread and of wine remain[45] — derives from the celebration of the sacrifice and is directed towards communion, both sacramental and spiritual.[46] It is the responsibility of pastors to encourage, also by their personal witness, the practice of Eucharistic adoration, and exposition of the Blessed Sacrament in particular, as well as prayer of adoration before Christ present under the Eucharistic species.[47]

It is pleasant to spend time with him, to lie close to his breast like the Beloved Disciple (cf. Jn 13:25) and to feel the infinite love present in his heart. If in our time Christians must be distinguished above all by the "art of prayer,"[48] how can we not feel a renewed need to spend time in spiritual converse, in silent adoration, in heartfelt love before Christ present in the Most Holy Sacrament? How often, dear brother and sisters, have I experienced this, and drawn from it strength, consolation, and support!

This practice, repeatedly praised and recommended by the Magisterium,[49] is supported by the example of many saints. Particularly outstanding in this regard was St. Alphonsus Liguori, who wrote, "Of all devotions, that of adoring Jesus in the Blessed Sacrament is the greatest after the sacraments, the one dearest to God and the one most helpful to us."[50] The Eucharist is a priceless treasure: By not only celebrating it but also by praying before it outside of Mass we are enabled to make contact with the very wellspring of grace. A Christian community desirous of contemplating the face of Christ in the spirit which I proposed in the apostolic letters *Novo Millennio Ineunte* and *Rosarium Virginis Mariae* cannot fail also to develop this aspect of Eucharistic worship, which prolongs and increases the fruits of our communion in the Body and Blood of the Lord.

THE APOSTOLICITY OF THE EUCHARIST AND OF THE CHURCH

26. If, as I have said, the Eucharist builds the Church and the Church makes the Eucharist, it follows that there is a profound relationship between the two, so much so that we can apply to the Eucharistic mystery the very words with which, in the Nicene-Constantinopolitan Creed, we profess the Church to be "one, holy, catholic and apostolic." The Eucharist, too, is one and catholic. It is also holy, indeed, the Most Holy Sacrament. But it is, above all, its apostolicity that we must now consider.

27. The *Catechism of the Catholic Church*, in explaining how the Church is apostolic — founded on the apostles — sees *three meanings* in this expression. First, "she was and remains built on 'the foundation of the apostles' (Eph 2:20), the witnesses chosen and sent on mission by Christ himself."[51] The Eucharist, too, has its foundation in the apostles, not in the sense that it did not originate in Christ himself, but because it was entrusted by Jesus to the apostles and has been handed down to us by them and by their successors. It is in continuity with the practice of the apostles, in obedience to the Lord's command, that the Church has celebrated the Eucharist down the centuries.

The second sense in which the Church is apostolic, as the *Catechism* points out, is that "with the help of the Spirit dwelling in her, the Church keeps and hands on the teaching, the 'good deposit,' the salutary words she has heard from the apostles."[52] Here, too, the Eucharist is apostolic, for it is celebrated in conformity with the faith of the apostles. At various times in the two-thousand-year history of the People of the New Covenant, the Church's Magisterium has more precisely defined her teaching on the Eucharist, including its proper terminology, precisely in order to safeguard the apostolic faith with regard to this sublime mystery. This faith remains unchanged, and it is essential for the Church that it remain unchanged.

28. Lastly, the Church is apostolic in the sense that she "continues to be taught, sanctified and guided by the apostles until Christ's return, through their successors in pastoral office: the college of bishops assisted by priests, in union with the Successor of Peter, the Church's supreme pastor."[53] Succession to the apostles in the pastoral mission necessarily entails the Sacrament of Holy Orders — that is, the uninterrupted sequence, from the very beginning, of valid episcopal ordinations.[54] This succession is essential for the Church to exist in a proper and full sense.

The Eucharist also expresses this sense of apostolicity. As the Second Vatican Council teaches, "the faithful join in the offering of the Eucharist by virtue of their royal priesthood,"[55] yet it is the ordained priest who, "acting in the person of Christ, brings about the Eucharistic Sacrifice and offers it to God in the name of all the people."[56] For this reason, the Roman Missal prescribes that only the priest should recite the Eucharistic prayer, while the people participate in faith and in silence.[57]

29. The expression repeatedly employed by the Second Vatican Council, according to which "the ministerial priest, acting in the person of Christ, brings about the Eucharistic Sacrifice,"[58] was already firmly rooted in papal teaching.[59] As I have pointed out on other occasions, the phrase *in persona Christi* "means more than offering 'in the name of' or 'in the place of' Christ. *In persona* means in specific sacramental identification with the eternal High Priest who is the author and principal subject of this sacrifice of his, a sacrifice in which, in truth, nobody can take his place."[60] The ministry of priests who have received the Sacrament of Holy Orders, in the economy of salvation chosen by Christ, makes clear that the Eucharist which they celebrate is *a gift which radically transcends the power of the assembly* and is in any event essential for validly linking the Eucharistic consecration to the sacrifice of the Cross and to the Last Supper. The assembly gathered together for the celebration of the Eucharist, if it is to be a truly Eucharistic assembly, absolutely requires the presence of an ordained priest as its president. ... The community is by itself incapable of providing an ordained minister. [The priest] minister is a gift which the assembly *receives through episcopal succession going back to the apostles*. It is the bishop who, through the Sacrament of Holy Orders, makes a new presbyter by conferring upon him the power to consecrate the Eucharist. Consequently,

"the Eucharistic mystery cannot be celebrated in any community except by an ordained priest, as the Fourth Lateran Council expressly taught."[61]

30. The Catholic Church's teaching on the relationship between priestly ministry and the Eucharist and her teaching on the Eucharistic Sacrifice have both been the subject in recent decades of a fruitful dialogue *in the area of ecumenism*. We must give thanks to the Blessed Trinity for the significant progress and convergence achieved in this regard, which lead us to hope one day for a full sharing of faith. Nonetheless, the observations of the council concerning the ecclesial communities which arose in the West from the sixteenth century onward and are separated from the Catholic Church remain fully pertinent: "The ecclesial communities separated from us lack that fullness of unity with us which should flow from baptism, and we believe that especially because of the lack of the Sacrament of [Holy] Orders they have not preserved the genuine and total reality of the Eucharistic mystery. Nevertheless, when they commemorate the Lord's death and resurrection in the Holy Supper, they profess that it signifies life in communion with Christ and they await his coming in glory."[62]

The Catholic faithful, therefore, while respecting the religious convictions of these separated brethren, must refrain from receiving the Communion distributed in their celebrations, so as not to condone an ambiguity about the nature of the Eucharist and, consequently, to fail in their duty to bear clear witness to the truth. This would result in slowing the progress being made toward full visible unity. Similarly, it is unthinkable to substitute for Sunday Mass ecumenical celebrations of the word or services of common prayer with Christians from the aforementioned ecclesial communities, or even participation in their own liturgical services. Such celebrations and services, however praiseworthy in certain situations, prepare for the goal of full communion, including Eucharistic communion, but they cannot replace it.

The fact that the power of consecrating the Eucharist has been entrusted only to bishops and priests does not represent any kind of belittlement of the rest of the People of God, for in the communion of the one Body of Christ which is the Church this gift redounds to the benefit of all.

31. If the Eucharist is the center and summit of the Church's life, it is likewise the center and summit of priestly ministry. For this reason, with a heart filled with gratitude to our Lord Jesus Christ, I repeat that the Eucharist "is the principal and central raison d'être of the sacrament of priesthood, which effectively came into being at the moment of the institution of the Eucharist."[63]

Priests are engaged in a wide variety of pastoral activities. If we also consider the social and cultural conditions of the modern world it is easy to understand how priests face the very real *risk of losing their focus* amid such a great number of different tasks. The Second Vatican Council saw in pastoral charity the bond which gives unity to the priest's life and work. This, the council adds, "flows mainly from the Eucharistic Sacrifice, which is therefore the center and root of the whole priestly life."[64] We can understand, then, how important it is for the spiritual life of the priest, as well as for the good of the Church and the world, that priests follow the council's recommendation to celebrate the Eucharist daily: "for even if the faithful are unable to be present, it is an act of Christ and the Church."[65] In this way priests will be able to counteract the daily tensions which lead to a lack of focus and they will find in the Eucharistic Sacrifice — the true center of their lives and ministry — the spiritual strength needed to deal with their different pastoral responsibilities. Their daily activity will thus become truly Eucharistic.

The centrality of the Eucharist in the life and ministry of priests is the basis of its centrality in the *pastoral promotion of priestly vocations*. It is in the Eucharist that prayer for vocations is most closely united to the prayer of Christ the Eternal High Priest. At the same time the diligence of priests in carrying out their Eucharistic ministry, together with the conscious, active, and fruitful participation of the faithful in the Eucharist, provides young men with a powerful example and incentive for responding generously to God's call. Often it is the example of a priest's fervent pastoral charity which the Lord uses to sow and to bring to fruition in a young man's heart the seed of a priestly calling.

32. All of this shows how distressing and irregular is the situation of a Christian community which, despite

having sufficient numbers and variety of faithful to form a parish, does not have a priest to lead it. Parishes are communities of the baptized who express and affirm their identity above all through the celebration of the Eucharistic Sacrifice. But this requires the presence of a presbyter, who alone is qualified to offer the Eucharist *in persona Christi*. When a community lacks a priest, attempts are rightly made somehow to remedy the situation so that it can continue its Sunday celebrations, and those religious and laity who lead their brothers and sisters in prayer exercise in a praiseworthy way the common priesthood of all the faithful based on the grace of baptism. But such solutions must be considered merely temporary, while the community awaits a priest.

The sacramental incompleteness of these celebrations should above all inspire the whole community to pray with greater fervor that the Lord will send laborers into his harvest (cf. Mt 9:38). It should also be an incentive to mobilize all the resources needed for an adequate pastoral promotion of vocations, without yielding to the temptation to seek solutions which lower the moral and formative standards demanded of candidates for the priesthood.

33. When, due to the scarcity of priests, non-ordained members of the faithful are entrusted with a share in the pastoral care of a parish, they should bear in mind that — as the Second Vatican Council teaches — "no Christian community can be built up unless it has its basis and center in the celebration of the Most Holy Eucharist."[66] They have a responsibility, therefore, to keep

alive in the community a genuine "hunger" for the Eucharist, so that no opportunity for the celebration of Mass will ever be missed, also taking advantage of the occasional presence of a priest who is not impeded by Church law from celebrating Mass.

CHAPTER FOUR
THE EUCHARIST AND ECCLESIAL COMMUNION

34. The Extraordinary Assembly of the Synod of Bishops in 1985 saw in the concept of an "ecclesiology of communion" the central and fundamental idea of the documents of the Second Vatican Council.[67] The Church is called during her earthly pilgrimage to maintain and promote communion with the Triune God and communion among the faithful. For this purpose, she possesses the word and the sacraments, particularly the Eucharist, by which she "constantly lives and grows"[68] and in which she expresses her very nature. It is not by chance that the term *communion* has become one of the names given to this sublime sacrament.

The Eucharist thus appears as the culmination of all the sacraments in perfecting our communion with God the Father by identification with his only begotten Son through the working of the Holy Spirit. With discerning faith a distinguished writer of the Byzantine tradition voiced this truth: in the Eucharist "unlike any other sacrament, the mystery [of communion] is so perfect that it brings us to the heights of every good thing: here is the ultimate goal of every human desire, because here we attain God and God joins himself to us in the most perfect union."[69] Precisely for this reason it is good to *cultivate in our hearts a constant desire for the sacrament of the Eucharist.* This was the origin of the practice of "spiritual communion," which has happily been established in the Church for centuries and recommended by saints who were masters of the spiritual life. St. Teresa of Jesus wrote, "When you do not receive Communion and you do not attend Mass, you can make a spiritual communion, which is a most beneficial practice; by it the love of God will be greatly impressed on you."[70]

35. The celebration of the Eucharist, however, cannot be the starting point for communion; it presupposes that communion already exists, a communion which it seeks to consolidate and bring to perfection. The sacrament is an expression of this bond of communion both in its *invisible* dimension, which, in Christ and through the working of the Holy Spirit, unites us to the Father and among ourselves, and in its *visible* dimension, which entails communion in the teaching of the apostles, in the sacraments, and in the Church's hierarchical order. The profound relationship between the invisible and the visible elements of ecclesial communion is constitutive of the Church as the sacrament of salvation.[71] Only in this context can there be a legitimate celebration of the Eucharist and true participation in it. Consequently, it is an intrinsic requirement of the Eucharist that it should be celebrated in communion, and specifically maintaining the various bonds of that communion intact.

36. Invisible communion, though by its nature always growing, presupposes the life of grace, by which we become "partakers of the divine nature" (2 Pt 1:4), and

the practice of the virtues of faith, hope, and love. Only in this way do we have true communion with the Father, the Son, and the Holy Spirit. Nor is faith sufficient; we must persevere in sanctifying grace and love, remaining within the Church "bodily" as well as "in our heart";[72] what is required, in the words of Saint Paul, is "faith working through love" (Gal 5:6).

Keeping these invisible bonds intact is a specific moral duty incumbent upon Christians who wish to participate fully in the Eucharist by receiving the Body and Blood of Christ. The apostle Paul appeals to this duty when he warns, "Let a man examine himself, and so eat of the bread and drink of the cup" (1 Cor 11:28). St. John Chrysostom, with his stirring eloquence, exhorted the faithful: "I too raise my voice, I beseech, beg, and implore that no one draw near to this sacred table with a sullied and corrupt conscience. Such an act, in fact, can never be called 'communion,' not even were we to touch the Lord's body a thousand times over, but 'condemnation,' 'torment,' and 'increase of punishment.'"[73]

Along these same lines, the *Catechism of the Catholic Church* rightly stipulates that "anyone conscious of a grave sin must receive the Sacrament of Reconciliation before coming to Communion."[74] I therefore desire to reaffirm that in the Church there remains in force, now and in the future, the rule by which the Council of Trent gave concrete expression to the apostle Paul's stern warning when it affirmed that, in order to receive the Eucharist in a worthy manner, "one must first confess one's sins, when one is aware of mortal sin."[75]

37. The two Sacraments of the Eucharist and Penance are very closely connected. Because the Eucharist makes present the redeeming sacrifice of the cross, perpetuating it sacramentally, it naturally gives rise to a continuous need for conversion, for a personal response to the appeal made by Saint Paul to the Christians of Corinth: "We beseech you on behalf of Christ, be reconciled to God" (2 Cor 5:20). If a Christian's conscience is burdened by serious sin, then the path of penance through the Sacrament of Reconciliation becomes necessary for full participation in the Eucharistic Sacrifice.

The judgment of one's state of grace obviously belongs only to the person involved, since it is a question of examining one's conscience. However, in cases of outward conduct which is seriously, clearly, and steadfastly contrary to the moral norm, the Church, in her pastoral concern for the good order of the community and out of respect for the sacrament, cannot fail to feel directly involved. The *Code of Canon Law* refers to this situation of a manifest lack of proper moral disposition when it states that those who "obstinately persist in manifest grave sin" are not to be admitted to Eucharistic communion.[76]

38. Ecclesial communion, as I have said, is likewise *visible*, and finds expression in the series of "bonds" listed by the council when it teaches, "They are fully incorporated into the society of the Church who, possessing the Spirit of Christ, accept her whole structure and all the means of salvation established within her, and within her visible framework are united to Christ, who governs

her through the supreme pontiff and the bishops, by the bonds of profession of faith, the sacraments, ecclesiastical government, and communion."[77]

The Eucharist, as the supreme sacramental manifestation of communion in the Church, demands to be celebrated in *a context where the outward bonds of communion are also intact.* In a special way, since the Eucharist is "as it were the summit of the spiritual life and the goal of all the sacraments,"[78] it requires that the bonds of communion in the sacraments, particularly in baptism and in priestly orders, be real. It is not possible to give Communion to a person who is not baptized or to one who rejects the full truth of the faith regarding the Eucharistic mystery. Christ is the truth, and he bears witness to the truth (cf. Jn 14:6; 18:37); the sacrament of his Body and Blood does not permit duplicity.

39. Furthermore, given the very nature of ecclesial communion and its relation to the Sacrament of the Eucharist, it must be recalled that "the Eucharistic Sacrifice, while always offered in a particular community, is never a celebration of that community alone. In fact, the community, in receiving the Eucharistic presence of the Lord, receives the entire gift of salvation and shows, even in its lasting visible particular form, that it is the image and true presence of the one, holy, catholic, and apostolic Church."[79] From this it follows that a truly Eucharistic community cannot be closed in upon itself, as though it were somehow self-sufficient; rather it must persevere in harmony with every other Catholic community.

The ecclesial communion of the Eucharistic assembly is a communion with its own *bishop* and with the *Roman pontiff*. The bishop, in effect, is the *visible* principle and the foundation of unity within his particular Church.[80] It would therefore be a great contradiction if the sacrament *par excellence* of the Church's unity were celebrated without true communion with the bishop. As St. Ignatius of Antioch wrote: "That Eucharist which is celebrated under the bishop, or under one to whom the bishop has given this charge, may be considered certain."[81] Likewise, since "the Roman pontiff, as the successor of Peter, is the perpetual and visible source and foundation of the unity of the bishops and of the multitude of the faithful,"[82] communion with him is intrinsically required for the celebration of the Eucharistic Sacrifice. Hence the great truth expressed which the liturgy expresses in a variety of ways: "Every celebration of the Eucharist is performed in union not only with the proper bishop, but also with the pope, with the episcopal order, with all the clergy, and with the entire people. Every valid celebration of the Eucharist expresses this universal communion with Peter and with the whole Church, or objectively calls for it, as in the case of the Christian churches separated from Rome."[83]

40. The Eucharist *creates communion* and *fosters communion*. Saint Paul wrote to the faithful of Corinth explaining how their divisions, reflected in their Eucharistic gatherings, contradicted what they were celebrating, the Lord's Supper. The apostle then urged them to reflect on the true reality of the Eucharist in order to return to the spirit of fraternal communion (cf. 1 Cor 11:17–34).

Saint Augustine effectively echoed this call when, in re-calling the apostle's words, "You are the body of Christ and individually members of it" (1 Cor 12:27), he went on to say: "If you are his body and members of him, then you will find set on the Lord's table your own mystery. Yes, you receive your own mystery."[84] And from this ob-servation he concludes: "Christ the Lord ... hallowed at his table the mystery of our peace and unity. Whoever receives the mystery of unity without preserving the bonds of peace receives not a mystery for his benefit but evidence against himself."[85]

41. The Eucharist's particular effectiveness in promot-ing communion is one of the reasons for the importance of Sunday Mass. I have already dwelt on this and on the other reasons which make Sunday Mass fundamental for the life of the Church and of individual believers in my apostolic letter on the sanctification of Sunday, *Dies Domini*.[86] There I recalled that the faithful have the ob-ligation to attend Mass, unless they are seriously im-peded, and that pastors have the corresponding duty to see that it is practical and possible for all to fulfill this precept.[87] More recently, in ... *Novo Millennio Ineunte*, in setting forth the pastoral path which the Church must take at the beginning of the third millennium, I drew particular attention to the Sunday Eucharist, emphasiz-ing its effectiveness for building communion. "It is," I wrote, "the privileged place where communion is cease-lessly proclaimed and nurtured. Precisely through shar-ing in the Eucharist, *the Lord's Day* also becomes *the Day of the Church*, when she can effectively exercise her role as the sacrament of unity."[88]

42. The safeguarding and promotion of ecclesial communion is a task of each member of the faithful, who finds in the Eucharist, as the sacrament of the Church's unity, an area of special concern. More specifically, this task is the particular responsibility of the Church's pastors, each according to his rank and ecclesiastical office. For this reason, the Church has drawn up norms aimed both at fostering the frequent and fruitful access of the faithful to the Eucharistic table and at determining the objective conditions under which Communion may not be given. The care shown in promoting the faithful observance of these norms becomes a practical means of showing love for the Eucharist and for the Church.

43. In considering the Eucharist as the sacrament of ecclesial communion, there is one subject which, due to its importance, must not be overlooked: I am referring to the *relationship of the Eucharist to ecumenical activity*. We should all give thanks to the Blessed Trinity for the many members of the faithful throughout the world who in recent decades have felt an ardent desire for unity among all Christians. The Second Vatican Council, at the beginning of its Decree on Ecumenism, sees this as a special gift of God.[89] It was an efficacious grace which inspired us, the sons and daughters of the Catholic Church, and our brothers and sisters from other churches and ecclesial communities, to set forth on the path of ecumenism.

Our longing for the goal of unity prompts us to turn to the Eucharist, which is the supreme sacrament of the unity of the People of God, in as much as it is the apt expression and the unsurpassable source of that unity.[90] In the celebration of the Eucharistic Sacrifice the Church prays that God, the Father of Mercies, will grant his children the fullness of the Holy Spirit so that they may become one body and one spirit in Christ.[91] In raising this prayer to the Father of Lights, from whom comes every good endowment and every perfect gift (cf. Jas 1:17), the Church believes that she will be heard, for she prays in union with Christ her Head and Spouse, who takes up this plea of his Bride and joins it to that of his own redemptive sacrifice.

44. Precisely because the Church's unity, which the Eucharist brings about through the Lord's sacrifice and by communion in his Body and Blood, absolutely requires full communion in the bonds of the profession of faith, the sacraments, and ecclesiastical governance, it is not possible to celebrate together the same Eucharistic liturgy until those bonds are fully reestablished. Any such concelebration would not be a valid means, and might well prove instead to be *an obstacle, to the attainment of full communion,* by weakening the sense of how far we remain from this goal and by introducing or exacerbating ambiguities with regard to one or another truth of the Faith. The path toward full unity can only be undertaken in truth. In this area, the prohibitions of Church law leave no room for uncertainty,[92] in fidelity to the moral norm laid down by the Second Vatican Council.[93]

I would like nonetheless to reaffirm what I said in my encyclical letter *Ut Unum Sint* after having acknowledged the impossibility of Eucharistic sharing: "And yet we do have a burning desire to join in celebrating the one Eucharist of the Lord, and this desire itself is already a common prayer of praise, a single supplication. Together we speak to the Father, and increasingly we do so 'with one heart.'"[94]

45. While it is never legitimate to concelebrate in the absence of full communion, the same is not true with respect to the administration of the Eucharist *under special circumstances, to individual persons* belonging to churches or ecclesial communities not in full communion with the Catholic Church. In this case, in fact, the intention is to meet a grave spiritual need for the eternal salvation of an individual believer, not to bring about an *intercommunion* which remains impossible until the visible bonds of ecclesial communion are fully reestablished.

This was the approach taken by the Second Vatican Council when it gave guidelines for responding to Eastern Christians separated in good faith from the Catholic Church who spontaneously ask to receive the Eucharist from a Catholic minister and are properly disposed.[95] This approach was then ratified by both Codes, which also consider — with necessary modifications — the case of other non-Eastern Christians who are not in full communion with the Catholic Church.[96]

46. In ... *Ut Unum Sint* I expressed my own appreciation of these norms, which make it possible to provide for the salvation of souls with proper discernment: "It is a source of joy to note that Catholic ministers are able, in

certain particular cases, to administer the Sacraments of the Eucharist, Penance, and the Anointing of the Sick to Christians who are not in full communion with the Catholic Church but who greatly desire to receive these sacraments, freely request them and manifest the faith which the Catholic Church professes with regard to these sacraments. Conversely, in specific cases and in particular circumstances, Catholics too can request these same sacraments from ministers of churches in which these sacraments are valid."[97]

These conditions, from which no dispensation can be given, must be carefully respected, even though they deal with specific individual cases, because the denial of one or more truths of the Faith regarding these sacraments and, among these, the truth regarding the need of the ministerial priesthood for their validity, renders the person asking improperly disposed to legitimately receiving them. And the opposite is also true: Catholics may not receive communion in those communities which lack a valid Sacrament of [Holy] Orders.[98]

The faithful observance of the body of norms established in this area[99] is a manifestation and, at the same time, a guarantee of our love for Jesus Christ in the Blessed Sacrament, for our brothers and sisters of different Christian confessions — who have a right to our witness to the truth — and for the cause itself of the promotion of unity.

THE DIGNITY
OF THE EUCHARISTIC
CELEBRATION

47. Reading the account of the institution of the Eucharist in the Synoptic Gospels, we are struck by the simplicity and the "solemnity" with which Jesus, on the evening of the Last Supper, instituted this great Sacrament. There is an episode which in some way serves as its prelude: *the anointing at Bethany*. A woman, whom John identifies as Mary, the sister of Lazarus, pours a flask of *costly ointment* over Jesus' head, which provokes from the disciples — and from Judas in particular (cf. Mt 26:8; Mk 14:4; Jn 12:4) — an indignant response, as if this act, in light of the needs of the poor, represented an intolerable "waste." But Jesus' own reaction is completely different. While in no way detracting from the duty of charity toward the needy, for whom the disciples must always show special care — "the poor you will always have with you" (Mt 26:11; Mk 14:7; cf. Jn 12:8) — he looks toward his imminent death and burial, and sees this act of anointing as an anticipation of the honor which his Body will continue to merit even after his death, indissolubly bound as it is to the mystery of his person.

The account continues, in the Synoptic Gospels, with

Jesus' charge to the disciples to *prepare carefully the "large upper room"* needed for the Passover meal (cf. Mk 14:15; Lk 22:12) and with the narration of the institution of the Eucharist. Reflecting at least in part the *Jewish rites* of the Passover meal leading up to the singing of the Hallel (cf. Mt 26:30; Mk 14:26), the story presents with sobriety and solemnity, even in the variants of the different traditions, the words spoken by Christ over the bread and wine, which he made into concrete expressions of the handing over of his Body and the shedding of his Blood. All these details are recorded by the evangelists in the light of a praxis of the "breaking of the bread" already well-established in the early Church. But certainly, from the time of Jesus on, the event of Holy Thursday has shown visible traces of a liturgical "sensibility" shaped by Old Testament tradition and open to being reshaped in Christian celebrations in a way consonant with the new content of Easter.

48. Like the woman who anointed Jesus in Bethany, *the Church has feared no "extravagance,"* devoting the best of her resources to expressing her wonder and adoration before the *unsurpassable gift of the Eucharist.* No less than the first disciples charged with preparing the "large upper room," [the Church] has felt the need, down the centuries and in her encounters with different cultures, to celebrate the Eucharist in a setting worthy of so great a mystery. In the wake of Jesus' own words and actions, and building upon the ritual heritage of Judaism, the *Christian liturgy was born.* Could there ever be an adequate means of expressing the acceptance of that self-gift which the divine Bridegroom continually

makes to his Bride, the Church, by bringing the Sacrifice offered once and for all on the cross to successive generations of believers and thus becoming nourishment for all the faithful? Though the idea of a "banquet" naturally suggests familiarity, the Church has never yielded to the temptation to trivialize this "intimacy" with her Spouse by forgetting that he is also her Lord and that the "banquet" always remains a sacrificial banquet marked by the Blood shed on Golgotha. *The Eucharistic Banquet is truly a "sacred" banquet* in which the simplicity of the signs conceals the unfathomable holiness of God: *O sacrum convivium, in quo Christus sumitur!* The bread which is broken on our altars, offered to us as wayfarers along the paths of the world, is *panis angelorum*, the bread of angels, which cannot be approached except with the humility of the centurion in the Gospel: "Lord, I am not worthy to have you come under my roof" (Mt 8:8; Lk 7:6).

49. With this heightened sense of mystery, we understand how the faith of the Church in the mystery of the Eucharist has found historical expression not only in the demand for an interior disposition of devotion, but also *in outward forms* meant to evoke and emphasize the grandeur of the event being celebrated. This led progressively to the development of *a particular form of regulating the Eucharistic liturgy,* with due respect for the various legitimately constituted ecclesial traditions. On this foundation *a rich artistic heritage* also developed. Architecture, sculpture, painting, and music, moved by the Christian mystery, have found in the Eucharist, both directly and indirectly, a source of great inspiration.

Such was the case, for example, with architecture, which witnessed the transition, once the historical situation made it possible, from the first places of Eucharistic celebration in the *domus*, or "homes," of Christian families to the solemn *basilicas* of the early centuries, to the imposing *cathedrals* of the Middle Ages, and to the *churches*, large and small, which gradually sprang up throughout the lands touched by Christianity. The designs of altars and tabernacles within church interiors were often not simply motivated by artistic inspiration, but also by a clear understanding of the mystery. The same could be said for *sacred music*, if we but think of the inspired Gregorian melodies and the many, often great, composers who sought to do justice to the liturgical texts of the Mass. Similarly, can we overlook the enormous quantity of *artistic production*, ranging from fine craftsmanship to authentic works of art, in the area of Church furnishings and vestments used for the celebration of the Eucharist?

It can be said that the Eucharist, while shaping the Church and her spirituality, has also powerfully affected "culture," and the arts in particular.

50. In this effort to adore the mystery grasped in its ritual and aesthetic dimensions, a certain "competition" has taken place between Christians of the West and the East. How could we not give particular thanks to the Lord for the contributions to Christian art made by the great architectural and artistic works of the Greco-Byzantine tradition and of the whole geographical area marked by Slav culture? In the East, sacred art has pre-

served a remarkably powerful sense of mystery, which leads artists to see their efforts at creating beauty not simply as an expression of their own talents, but also as *a genuine service to the Faith*. Passing well beyond mere technical skill, they have shown themselves docile and open to the inspiration of the Holy Spirit.

The architectural and mosaic splendors of the Christian East and West are a patrimony belonging to all believers; they contain a hope, and even a pledge, of the desired fullness of communion in faith and in celebration. This would presuppose and demand, as in Andrei Rublev's famous depiction of the Trinity, *a profoundly Eucharistic Church* in which the presence of the mystery of Christ in the broken bread is as it were immersed in the ineffable unity of the three divine Persons, making of the Church herself an "icon" of the Trinity.

Within this context of an art aimed at expressing, in all its elements, the meaning of the Eucharist in accordance with the Church's teaching, attention needs to be given to the norms regulating *the construction and decor of sacred buildings*. As history shows, and as I emphasized in my *Letter to Artists*,[100] the Church has always left ample room for the creativity of artists. But sacred art must be outstanding for its ability to express adequately the mystery grasped in the fullness of the Church's faith and in accordance with the pastoral guidelines appropriately laid down by competent authority. This holds true both for the figurative arts and for sacred music.

51. The development of sacred art and liturgical dis-

cipline which took place in lands of ancient Christian heritage is also taking place *on continents where Christianity is younger.* This was precisely the approach supported by the Second Vatican Council on the need for sound and proper "inculturation." In my numerous pastoral visits, I have seen, throughout the world, the great vitality which the celebration of the Eucharist can have when marked by the forms, styles, and sensibilities of different cultures. By adaptation to the changing conditions of time and place, the Eucharist offers sustenance not only to individuals but to entire peoples, and it shapes cultures inspired by Christianity.

It is necessary, however, that this important work of adaptation be carried out with a constant awareness of the ineffable mystery against which every generation is called to measure itself. The "treasure" is too important and precious to risk impoverishment or compromise through forms of experimentation or practices introduced without a careful review on the part of the competent ecclesiastical authorities. Furthermore, the centrality of the Eucharistic mystery demands that any such review must be undertaken in close association with the Holy See. As I wrote in my post-synodal apostolic exhortation *Ecclesia in Asia,* "such cooperation is essential because the Sacred Liturgy expresses and celebrates the one faith professed by all and, being the heritage of the whole Church, cannot be determined by local Churches in isolation from the universal Church."[101]

52. All of this makes clear the great responsibility which belongs to priests, in particular, for the celebration of

the Eucharist. It is their responsibility to preside at the Eucharist *in persona Christi* and to provide a witness to and a service of communion not only for the community directly taking part in the celebration, but also for the universal Church, which is a part of every Eucharist. It must be lamented that, especially in the years following the post-conciliar liturgical reform, as a result of a misguided sense of creativity and adaptation, there have been a number of *abuses* which have been a source of suffering for many. A certain reaction against "formalism" has led some, especially in certain regions, to consider the "forms" chosen by the Church's great liturgical tradition and her Magisterium as nonbinding and to introduce unauthorized innovations which are often completely inappropriate.

I consider it my duty, therefore, to appeal urgently that the liturgical norms for the celebration of the Eucharist be observed with great fidelity. These norms are a concrete expression of the authentically ecclesial nature of the Eucharist; this is their deepest meaning. Liturgy is never anyone's private property, be it of the celebrant or of the community in which the mysteries are celebrated. The apostle Paul had to address fiery words to the community of Corinth because of grave shortcomings in their celebration of the Eucharist, resulting in divisions (*schismata*) and the emergence of factions (*haireseis*) (cf. 1 Cor 11:17–34). Our time, too, calls for a renewed awareness and appreciation of liturgical norms as a reflection of, and a witness to, the one universal Church made present in every celebration of the Eucharist. Priests who faithfully celebrate Mass according to the liturgical norms, and communities which conform to those norms, quietly but eloquently demonstrate their love for the Church. Precisely to bring out more clearly this deeper meaning of liturgical norms, I have asked the competent offices of the Roman Curia to prepare a more specific document, including prescriptions of a juridical nature, on this very important subject. No one is permitted to undervalue the mystery entrusted to our hands: It is too great for anyone to feel free to treat it lightly and with disregard for its sacredness and its universality.

CHAPTER SIX

AT THE SCHOOL OF MARY, "WOMAN OF THE EUCHARIST"

53. If we wish to rediscover in all its richness the profound relationship between the Church and the Eucharist, we cannot neglect Mary, mother and model of the Church. In my apostolic letter *Rosarium Virginis Mariae*, I pointed to the Blessed Virgin Mary as our teacher in contemplating Christ's face, and among the mysteries of light I included *the institution of the Eucharist*.[102] Mary can guide us toward this most holy Sacrament, because she herself has a profound relationship with it.

At first glance, the Gospel is silent on this subject. The account of the institution of the Eucharist on the night of Holy Thursday makes no mention of Mary. Yet we know that she was present among the apostles who prayed "with one accord" (cf. Acts 1:14) *in the first community which gathered after the Ascension in expectation of Pentecost*. Certainly, Mary must have been present at the Eucharistic celebrations of the first generation of Christians, who were devoted to "the breaking of bread" (Acts 2:42).

But in addition to her sharing in the Eucharistic banquet, an indirect picture of Mary's relationship with the Eucharist can be had, beginning with her interior disposition. *Mary is a "woman of the Eucharist" in her whole life.* The Church, which looks to Mary as a model, is also called to imitate her in her relationship with this most holy mystery.

54. *Mysterium fidei!* If the Eucharist is a mystery of faith which so greatly transcends our understanding as to call for sheer abandonment to the word of God, then there can be no one like Mary to act as our support and guide in acquiring this disposition. In repeating what Christ did at the Last Supper in obedience to his command, "Do this in memory of me!", we also accept Mary's invitation to obey him without hesitation, "Do whatever he tells you" (Jn 2:5). With the same maternal concern which she showed at the wedding feast of Cana, Mary seems to say to us: "Do not waver; trust in the words of my Son. If he was able to change water into wine, he can also turn bread and wine into his Body and Blood, and through this mystery bestow on believers the living memorial of his passover, thus becoming the 'bread of life.'"

55. In a certain sense Mary lived her *Eucharistic faith* even before the institution of the Eucharist by the very fact that *she offered her virginal womb for the Incarnation of God's Word.* The Eucharist, while commemorating the passion and resurrection, is also in continuity with the Incarnation. At the Annunciation, Mary conceived the Son of God in the physical reality of his Body and Blood, thus anticipating within herself what to some degree happens sacramentally in every believer who receives, under the signs of bread and wine, the

Lord's Body and Blood.

As a result, there is a profound analogy between the *Fiat*, which Mary said in reply to the angel, and the *Amen*, which every believer says when receiving the body of the Lord. Mary was asked to believe that the One whom she conceived "through the Holy Spirit" was "the Son of God" (Lk 1:30–35). In continuity with the Virgin's faith, in the Eucharistic mystery we are asked to believe that the same Jesus Christ, Son of God and son of Mary, becomes present in his full humanity and divinity under the signs of bread and wine.

"Blessed is she who believed" (Lk 1:45). Mary also anticipated, in the mystery of the Incarnation, the Church's Eucharistic faith. When, at the Visitation, she bore in her womb the Word-made-Flesh, she became in some way a "tabernacle" — the first "tabernacle" in history — in which the Son of God, still invisible to our human gaze, allowed himself to be adored by Elizabeth, radiating his light as it were through the eyes and the voice of Mary. And is not the enraptured gaze of Mary as she contemplated the face of the newborn Christ and cradled him in her arms that unparalleled model of love which should inspire us every time we receive Eucharistic communion?

56. Mary, throughout her life at Christ's side, and not only on Calvary, made her own *the sacrificial dimension of the Eucharist*. When she brought the child Jesus to the Temple in Jerusalem "to present him to the Lord" (Lk 2:22), she heard the aged Simeon announce that

the child would be a "sign of contradiction" and that a sword would also pierce her own heart (cf. Lk 2:34–35). The tragedy of her son's crucifixion was thus foretold, and in some sense Mary's *Stabat Mater* at the foot of the cross was foreshadowed. In her daily preparation for Calvary, Mary experienced a kind of "anticipated Eucharist" — one might say a "spiritual communion" — of desire and of oblation, which would culminate in her union with her Son in his passion, and then find expression after Easter by her partaking in the Eucharist which the apostles celebrated as the memorial of that passion.

What must Mary have felt as she heard from the mouth of Peter, John, James, and the other apostles the words spoken at the Last Supper: "This is my body which is given for you" (Lk 22:19)? The body given up for us and made present under sacramental signs was the same body which she had conceived in her womb! For Mary, receiving the Eucharist must have somehow meant welcoming once more into her womb that heart which had beat in unison with hers and reliving what she had experienced at the foot of the cross.

57. "Do this in remembrance of me" (Lk 22:19). In the "memorial" of Calvary, all that Christ accomplished by his passion and his death is present. Consequently, *all that Christ did with regard to his mother* for our sake is also present. To her he gave the beloved disciple and, in him, each of us: "Behold, your Son!" To each of us he also says, "Behold your mother!" (cf. Jn 19:26–27).

Experiencing the memorial of Christ's death in the Eucharist also means continually receiving this gift. It means accepting — like John — the one who is given to us anew as our mother. It also means taking on a commitment to be conformed to Christ, putting ourselves at the school of his mother and allowing her to accompany us. Mary is present, with the Church and as Mother of the Church, at each of our celebrations of the Eucharist. If the Church and the Eucharist are inseparably united, the same ought to be said of Mary and the Eucharist. This is one reason why, since ancient times, the commemoration of Mary has always been part of the Eucharistic celebrations of the Churches of East and West.

58. In the Eucharist the Church is completely united to Christ and his sacrifice, and makes her own the spirit of Mary. This truth can be understood more deeply by *re-reading the Magnificat* in a Eucharistic key. The Eucharist, like the Canticle of Mary, is first and foremost praise and thanksgiving. When Mary exclaims, "My soul magnifies the Lord and my spirit rejoices in God my Savior," she already bears Jesus in her womb. She praises God "through" Jesus, but she also praises him "in" Jesus and "with" Jesus. This is itself the true "Eucharistic attitude."

At the same time Mary recalls the wonders worked by God in salvation history in fulfilment of the promise once made to the fathers (cf. Lk 1:55), and proclaims the wonder that surpasses them all, the redemptive incarnation. Lastly, the *Magnificat* reflects the eschatological tension of the Eucharist. Every time the Son of God comes again to us in the "poverty" of the sacramental signs of bread and wine, the seeds of that new history wherein the mighty are "put down from their thrones" and "those of low degree are exalted" (cf. Lk 1:52), take root in the world. Mary sings of the "new heavens" and the "new earth" which find in the Eucharist their anticipation and in some sense their program and plan. The *Magnificat* expresses Mary's spirituality, and there is nothing greater than this spirituality for helping us to experience the mystery of the Eucharist. The Eucharist has been given to us so that our life, like that of Mary, may become completely a *Magnificat!*

CONCLUSION

59. *Ave, verum corpus natum de Maria Virgine!* Several years ago, I celebrated the fiftieth anniversary of my priesthood. Today I have the grace of offering the Church this encyclical on the Eucharist on the Holy Thursday which falls *during the twenty-fifth year of my Petrine ministry.* As I do so, my heart is filled with gratitude. For over a half century, every day, beginning on November 2, 1946, when I celebrated my first Mass in the Crypt of Saint Leonard in Wawel Cathedral in Kraków, my eyes have gazed in recollection upon the host and the chalice, where time and space in some way "merge" and the drama of Golgotha is re-presented in a living way, thus revealing its mysterious "contemporaneity." Each day my faith has been able to recognize in the consecrated bread and wine the divine Wayfarer who joined the two disciples on the road to Emmaus and opened their eyes to the light and their hearts to new hope (cf. Lk 24:13–35).

Allow me, dear brothers and sisters, to share with deep emotion, as a means of accompanying and strengthening your faith, my own testimony of faith in the Most Holy Eucharist. *Ave verum corpus natum de Maria Virgine, vere passum, immolatum, in cruce pro homine!* Here is the Church's treasure, the heart of the world, the pledge of the fulfillment for which each man and woman, even unconsciously, yearns. A great and transcendent mystery, indeed, and one that taxes our mind's ability to pass beyond appearances. Here our senses fail us: *visus, tactus, gustus in te fallitur,* in the words of the hymn *Adoro Te Devote*; yet faith alone, rooted in the word of Christ handed down to us by the apostles, is sufficient for us. Allow me, like Peter at the end of the Eucharistic discourse in John's Gospel, to say once more to Christ, in the name of the whole Church and in the name of each of you: "Lord to whom shall we go? You have the words of eternal life" (Jn 6:68).

60. At the dawn of this third millennium, we, the children of the Church, are called to undertake with renewed enthusiasm the journey of Christian living. As I wrote in my apostolic letter *Novo Millennio Ineunte*: "It is not a matter of inventing a 'new program.' The program already exists: it is the plan found in the Gospel and in the living Tradition; it is the same as ever. Ultimately, it has its center in Christ himself, who is to be known, loved, and imitated, so that in him we may live the life of the Trinity, and with him transform history until its fulfillment in the heavenly Jerusalem."[103] The implementation of this program of a renewed impetus in Christian living passes through the Eucharist.

Every commitment to holiness, every activity aimed at carrying out the Church's mission, every work of pastoral planning, must draw the strength it needs from the Eucharistic mystery and in turn be directed to that mystery as its culmination. In the Eucharist we have Jesus, we have his redemptive sacrifice, we have his resurrection, we have the gift of the Holy Spirit, we have adoration, obedience, and love of the Father. Were we to disregard the Eucharist, how could we overcome our own deficiency?

Conclusion

61. The mystery of the Eucharist — sacrifice, presence, banquet — *does not allow for reduction or exploitation*; it must be experienced and lived in its integrity, both in its celebration and in the intimate converse with Jesus which takes place after receiving Communion or in a prayerful moment of Eucharistic adoration apart from Mass. These are times when the Church is firmly built up and it becomes clear what she truly is: one, holy, catholic, and apostolic; the people, temple, and family of God; the body and bride of Christ, enlivened by the Holy Spirit; the universal sacrament of salvation and a hierarchically structured communion.

The path taken by the Church in these first years of the third millennium is also a *path of renewed ecumenical commitment.* The final decades of the second millennium, culminating in the Great Jubilee, have spurred us along this path and called for all the baptized to respond to the prayer of Jesus *"ut unum sint"* (Jn 17:11). The path itself is long and strewn with obstacles greater than our human resources alone can overcome, yet we have the Eucharist, and in its presence we can hear in the depths of our hearts, as if they were addressed to us, the same words heard by the Prophet Elijah: "Arise and eat, else the journey will be too great for you" (1 Kgs 19:7). The treasure of the Eucharist, which the Lord places before us, impels us toward the goal of full sharing with all our brothers and sisters to whom we are joined by our common baptism. But if this treasure is not to be squandered, we need to respect the demands which derive from its being the sacrament of communion in faith and in apostolic succession.

By giving the Eucharist the prominence it deserves, and by being careful not to diminish any of its dimensions or demands, we show that we are truly conscious of the greatness of this gift. We are urged to do so by an uninterrupted tradition, which from the first centuries on has found the Christian community ever vigilant in guarding this "treasure." Inspired by love, the Church is anxious to hand on to future generations of Christians, without loss, her faith and teaching with regard to the mystery of the Eucharist. There can be no danger of excess in our care for this mystery, for "in this Sacrament is recapitulated the whole mystery of our salvation."[104]

62. Let us take our place, dear brothers and sisters, *at the school of the saints*, who are the great interpreters of true Eucharistic piety. In them the theology of the Eucharist takes on all the splendor of a lived reality; it becomes "contagious," and, in a manner of speaking, it "warms our hearts." Above all, let us *listen to Mary Most Holy*, in whom the mystery of the Eucharist appears, more than in anyone else, as a *mystery of light*. Gazing upon Mary, we come to know *the transforming power present in the Eucharist*. In her we see the world renewed in love. Contemplating her, assumed body and soul into heaven, we see opening up before us those "new heavens" and that "new earth" which will appear at the second coming of Christ. Here below, the Eucharist represents their pledge, and in a certain way, their anticipation: *"Veni, Domine Iesu!"* (Rv 22:20).

In the humble signs of bread and wine, changed into his Body and Blood, Christ walks beside us as our strength and our food for the journey, and he enables us to become, for everyone, witnesses of hope. If, in the presence of this mystery, reason experiences its limits, the heart, enlightened by the grace of the Holy Spirit, clearly sees the response that is demanded and bows low in adoration and unbounded love.

Let us make our own the words of St. Thomas Aquinas, an eminent theologian and an impassioned poet of Christ in the Eucharist, and turn in hope to the contemplation of that goal to which our hearts aspire in their thirst for joy and peace:

Bone pastor, panis vere,
Iesu, nostri miserere ...

Come then, good Shepherd, bread divine,
Still show to us thy mercy sign;
Oh, feed us, still keep us thine;
So we may see thy glories shine
in fields of immortality.

O thou, the wisest, mightiest, best,
Our present food, our future rest,
Come, make us each thy chosen guest,
Co-heirs of thine, and comrades blest
With saints whose dwelling is with thee.

Given in Rome, at Saint Peter's, on April 17, Holy Thursday, in the year 2003, the twenty-fifth of my pontificate, the Year of the Rosary.

IOANNES PAULUS II

NOTES

1. Second Vatican Council, Dogmatic Constitution on the Church, *Lumen Gentium*, 11.

2. Second Vatican Council, Decree on the Ministry and Life of Priests. *Presbyterorum Ordinis*, 5.

3. Cf. John Paul II, apostolic letter *Rosarium Virginis Mariae* (October 16, 2002), 21: AAS 95 (2003), 19.

4. This is the title which I gave to an autobiographical testimony issued for my fiftieth anniversary of priestly ordination.

5. *Leonis XIII P.M. Acta*, XXII (1903), 115–136.

6. AAS 39 (1947), 521–595.

7. AAS 57 (1965), 753–774.

8. AAS 72 (1980), 113–148.

9. Cf. Second Vatican Council, Constitution on the Sacred Liturgy, *Sacrosanctum Concilium*, 47: "Our Savior instituted the Eucharistic Sacrifice of his body and blood, in order to perpetuate the sacrifice of the Cross throughout time, until he should return."

10. *Catechism of the Catholic Church*, 1085.

11. Second Vatican Council, *Lumen Gentium*, 3.

12. Cf. Paul VI, *Solemn Profession of Faith*, June 30, 1968, 24: AAS 60 (1968), 442; John Paul II, apostolic letter *Dominicae Cenae* (February 24, 1980), 12: AAS 72 (1980), 142.

13. *Catechism of the Catholic Church*, 1382.

14. Ibid., 1367.

15. *In Epistolam ad Hebraeos Homiliae*, Hom. 17,3: PG 63, 131.

16. Cf. Council of Trent, Session XXII, *Doctrina de ss. Missae Sacrificio*, Chapter 2: DS 1743: "It is one and the same victim here offering himself by the ministry of his priests, who then offered himself on the cross; it is only the manner of offering that is different."

17. Pius XII, encyclical letter *Mediator Dei* (November 20, 1947): AAS 39 (1947), 548.

18. John Paul II, encyclical letter *Redemptor Hominis* (March 15, 1979), 20: AAS 71 (1979), 310.

19. *Lumen Gentium*, 11.

20. *De Sacramentis*, V, 4, 26: CSEL 73, 70.

21. *In Ioannis Evangelium*, XII, 20: PG 74, 726.

22. Paul VI, encyclical letter *Mysterium Fidei* (September 3, 1965): AAS 57 (1965), 764.

23. Session XIII, *Decretum de ss. Eucharistia*, Chapter 4: DS 1642.

24. *Mystagogical Catecheses*, IV, 6: SCh 126, 138.

25. Second Vatican Council, Dogmatic Constitution on Divine Revelation, *Dei Verbum*, 8.

26. *Solemn Profession of Faith*, June 30, 1968, 25: AAS 60 (1968), 442–443.

27. *Sermo IV in Hebdomadam Sanctam*: CSCO 413/Syr. 182, 55.

28. Anaphora.

29. Eucharistic Prayer III.

30. Solemnity of the Body and Blood of Christ, Second Vespers, Antiphon to the *Magnificat*.

31. *Missale Romanum*, embolism following the Lord's Prayer.

32. *Ad Ephesios*, 20: PG 5, 661.

33. Cf. Second Vatican Council, Pastoral Constitution on the Church in the Modern World, *Gaudium et Spes*, 39.

34. "Do you wish to honor the body of Christ? Do not ignore him when he is naked. Do not pay him homage in the temple clad in silk, only then to neglect him outside where he is cold and ill-clad. He who said: 'This is my body' is the same who said: 'You saw me hungry and you gave me no food,' and 'Whatever you did to the least of my brothers you did also to me.'... What good is it

if the Eucharistic table is overloaded with golden chalices when your brother is dying of hunger. Start by satisfying his hunger and then with what is left you may adorn the altar as well": St. John Chrysostom, *In Evangelium S. Matthaei,* hom. 50:3–4: PG 58, 508–509; cf. John Paul II, encyclical letter *Sollicitudo Rei Socialis* (December 30, 1987), 31: AAS 80 (1988), 553–556.

35. *Lumen Gentium,* 3.

36. Ibid.

37. Second Vatican Council, Decree on the Missionary Activity of the Church, *Ad Gentes,* 5.

38. "Moses took the blood and threw it upon the people, and said: 'Behold the blood of the covenant which the Lord has made with you in accordance with all these words'" (Ex 24:8).

39. Cf. *Lumen Gentium,* 1.

40. Cf. ibid., 9.

41. Cf. Second Vatican Council, Decree on the Life and Ministry of Priests, *Presbyterorum Ordinis,* 5. The same decree, in No. 6, says, "No Christian community can be built up which does not grow from and hinge on the celebration of the most holy Eucharist."

42. *In Epistolam I ad Corinthios Homiliae,* 24, 2: PG 61, 200; cf. *Didache,* IX, 4: F. X. Funk, I, 22; Saint Cyprian, *Ep.* LXIII, 13: PL 4, 384.

43. PO 26, 206.

44. *Lumen Gentium,* 1.

45. Cf. Council of Trent, Session XIII, *Decretum de ss. Eucharistia,* Canon 4: DS 1654.

46. Cf. *Rituale Romanum: De sacra communione et de cultu mysterii eucharistici extra Missam,* 36 (No. 80).

47. Cf. ibid., 38–39 (Nos. 86–90).

48. John Paul II, apostolic letter *Novo Millennio Ineunte* (January 6, 2001), 32: AAS 93 (2001), 288.

49. "In the course of the day the faithful should not omit visiting the Blessed Sacrament, which in accordance with liturgical law must be reserved in churches with great reverence in a prominent place. Such visits are a sign of gratitude, an expression of love and an acknowledgment of the Lord's presence": Paul VI, *Mysterium Fidei*: AAS 57 (1965), 771.

50. *Visite al SS. Sacramento e a Maria Santissima*, Introduction: *Opere Ascetiche*, Avellino, 2000, 295.

51. No. 857.

52. Ibid.

53. Ibid.

54. Cf. Congregation for the Doctrine of the Faith, letter *Sacerdotium Ministeriale* (August 6, 1983), III.2: AAS 75 (1983), 1005.

55. *Lumen Gentium*, 10.

56. Ibid.

57. Cf. *Institutio Generalis*: Editio typica tertia, No. 147.

58. Cf. *Lumen Gentium*, 10 and 28; *Presbyterorum Ordinis*, 2.

59. "The minister of the altar acts in the person of Christ inasmuch as he is head, making an offering in the name of all the members": Pius XII, *Mediator Dei*: AAS 39 (1947), 556; cf. Pius X, apostolic exhortation *Haerent Animo* (August 4, 1908): *Acta Pii X*, IV, 16; Pius XI, encyclical letter *Ad Catholici Sacerdotii* (December 20, 1935): AAS 28 (1936), 20.

60. Apostolic letter *Dominicae Cenae* (February 24, 1980), 8: AAS 72 (1980), 128–129.

61. Congregation for the Doctrine of the Faith, *Sacerdotium Ministeriale*, III.4: AAS 75 (1983), 1006; cf. Fourth Lateran Council, Chapter 1, Constitution on the Catholic Faith, *Firmiter Credimus*: DS 802.

62. Second Vatican Council, Decree on Ecumenism, *Unitatis Redintegratio*, 22.

63. *Dominicae Cenae*, 2: AAS 72 (1980), 115.

Notes

64. *Presbyterorum Ordinis*, 14.

65. Ibid., 13; cf. *Code of Canon Law*, Canon 904; *Code of Canons of the Eastern Churches*, Canon 378.

66. *Presbyterorum Ordinis*, 6.

67. Cf. Final Report, II.C.1: *L'Osservatore Romano*, December 10, 1985, 7.

68. Second Vatican Council, *Lumen Gentium*, 26.

69. Nicolas Cabasilas, *Life in Christ*, IV, 10: SCh 355, 270.

70. *Camino de Perfección*, Chapter 35.

71. Cf. Congregation for the Doctrine of the Faith, Letter to the Bishops of the Catholic Church on Some Aspects of the Church Understood as Communion *Communionis Notio* (May 28, 1992), 4: AAS 85 (1993), 839–840.

72. Cf. *Lumen Gentium*, 14.

73. *Homiliae in Isaiam*, 6, 3: PG 56, 139.

74. No. 1385; cf. *Code of Canon Law*, Canon 916; *Code of Canons of the Eastern Churches*, Canon 711.

75. Address to the Members of the Sacred Apostolic Penitentiary and the Penitentiaries of the Patriarchal Basilicas of Rome (30 January 1981): AAS 73 (1981), 203. Cf. Council of Trent, Sess. XIII, *Decretum de ss. Eucharistia*, Chapter 7 and Canon 11: DS 1647, 1661.

76. Canon 915; *Code of Canons of the Eastern Churches*, Canon 712.

77. *Lumen Gentium*, 14.

78. St. Thomas Aquinas, *Summa Theologiae*, III, q. 73, a. 3c.

79. Congregation for the Doctrine of the Faith, Letter to the Bishops of the Catholic Church on Some Aspects of the Church Understood as Communion, *Communionis Notio* (May 28, 1992), 11: AAS 85 (1993), 844.

80. Cf. *Lumen Gentium*, 23.

81. *Ad Smyrnaeos*, 8: PG 5, 713.

Notes

82. *Lumen Gentium*, 23.
83. Congregation for the Doctrine of the Faith, *Communionis Notio*, 14: AAS 85 (1993), 847.
84. *Sermo 272*: PL 38, 1247.
85. Ibid., 1248.
86. Cf. Nos. 31-51: AAS 90 (1998), 731-746.
87. Cf. ibid., Nos. 48-49: AAS 90 (1998), 744.
88. No. 36: AAS 93 (2001), 291-292.
89. Cf. *Unitatis Redintegratio*, 1.
90. Cf. *Lumen Gentium*, 11.
91. "Join all of us, who share the one bread and the one cup, to one another in the communion of the one Holy Spirit": *Anaphora of the Liturgy of Saint Basil*.
92. Cf. *Code of Canon Law*, Canon 908; *Code of Canons of the Eastern Churches*, Canon 702; Pontifical Council for the Promotion of Christian Unity, *Ecumenical Directory*, March 25, 1993, 122-125, 129-131: AAS 85 (1993), 1086-1089; Congregation for the Doctrine of the Faith, letter *Ad Exsequendam*, May 18, 2001: AAS 93 (2001), 786.
93. "Divine law forbids any common worship which would damage the unity of the Church, or involve formal acceptance of falsehood or the danger of deviation in the faith, of scandal, or of indifferentism": Second Vatican Council, Decree on the Eastern Catholic Churches, *Orientalium Ecclesiarum*, 26.
94. No. 45: AAS 87 (1995), 948.
95. *Orientalium Ecclesiarum*, 27.
96. Cf. *Code of Canon Law*, Canon 844 §§ 3-4; *Code of Canons of the Eastern Churches*, Canon 671 §§ 3-4.
97. No. 46: AAS 87 (1995), 948.
98. Cf. *Unitatis Redintegratio*, 22.
99. *Code of Canon Law*, Canon 844; *Code of Canons of the Eastern Churches*, Canon 671.

Notes

100. Cf. AAS 91 (1999), 1155–1172.
101. No. 22: AAS 92 (2000), 485.
102. Cf. No. 21: AAS 95 (2003), 20.
103. No. 29: AAS 93 (2001), 285.
104. Aquinas, *Summa Theologiae*, III, q. 83, a. 4c.